CW00497996

Dr Jekyll and Mr Hyde
25 Key Quotations for GCSE

Heather Hawkins

Series Editor: Hannah Rabey

firestonebooks.com

Dr Jekyll and Mr Hyde
25 Key Quotations for GCSE
Heather Hawkins

Series Editor: Hannah Rabey

Text © Heather Hawkins
About this Book section © Hannah Rabey

Cover © XL Book Cover Design
xlbookcoverdesign.co.uk

2021 Edition

ISBN-13: 978-1909608290

Published by Firestone Books

This guide is not endorsed by or affiliated with any
exam boards/awarding bodies.

firestonebooks.com

You can stay up to date by following Firestone Books on
Facebook and Twitter, or subscribing to our fabulous newsletter.
Go on – you know you want to…

Contents

About this Book

The GCSE English Literature exam relies on understanding a wide range of relevant references, studied both in lessons and as part of revision. This guide will provide you with in-depth analysis of 25 key quotations in Robert Louis Stevenson's novella *The Strange Case of Dr Jekyll and Mr Hyde*, written by experts to ensure that you are prepared for success.

In this guide you will find:

- A biography of Robert Louis Stevenson's life
- A summary of the key events in the novella
- Form in *Dr Jekyll and Mr Hyde*
- 25 key analysed quotations
- A key terms glossary (key terms are denoted by an asterisk)

The 25 quotations include:

- Detailed analysis of the quotation
- Key context relating to the quotation
- A list of key themes and characters that the quotation links to

A Biography of
Robert Louis Stevenson

Robert Louis Stevenson was born on 13 November 1850 in Edinburgh. His father, Thomas, was an engineer and his mother, Margaret, came from a family of lawyers. Stevenson did not enjoy good health from his childhood onwards, suffering bronchial infections and fevers, and eventually haemorrhaging of the lungs which confined him to bed. Unable to participate in usual childhood games, Stevenson developed a very vivid imagination from an early age, which was encouraged by his closeness to Alison Cunningham ('Cummy') who became Stevenson's nurse in 1852 and stayed with the family until 1872, when Stevenson was twenty-two years of age. Cummy held strong Calvinist* religious beliefs and told Stevenson many Biblical stories when he was confined to bed. The Calvinist belief is that sin is inherent in human nature and only overcome by a reliance upon Christ and repentance* of one's sinful nature. This notion of the capacity of humans to be evil is a key theme of *Dr Jekyll and Mr Hyde* and is characterised in Mr Hyde.

Stevenson spent his childhood in Edinburgh and enrolled at Edinburgh University in 1867 with the intention of studying engineering, but soon decided to study law instead. Although he was called to the Scottish Bar in 1875, Stevenson never practised as a lawyer but began to write travel articles for magazines based upon his own experiences abroad.

In 1876 Stevenson met his future wife, Fanny Osbourne, a thirty-six-year-old American who was separated from her husband and had an eight-year-old son. After publishing more travel writings, Stevenson joined Fanny in California and wrote *The Amateur Emigrant* which was eventually published in 1894. In 1880 Stevenson married Fanny once she had divorced her first husband.

1883 saw the publication of Stevenson's *Treasure Island*, a children's story which helped to establish Stevenson's reputation as a writer and remains popular today. Then, in 1884, Stevenson and Fanny moved to Bournemouth and Stevenson published *The Body Snatcher* for Christmas, following the Victorian tradition of spine-chilling ghost stories. *The Strange Case of Dr Jekyll and Mr Hyde* also follows in this tradition. The novella* was originally intended for publication at Christmas of 1885 but was withdrawn as the market was swamped and published in January 1886 instead. Stevenson's popularity gradually grew and in 1886 he wrote another of his famous works, *Kidnapped.*

In 1886 a stage production of *Dr Jekyll and Mr Hyde* opened in London, indicating the popularity of his novella, though the production was withdrawn out of sensitivity to the Whitechapel Murders which took place in East London at the time.

Stevenson continued his prolific output of works, writing 13 novels and novellas, five collections of travel writing, four collections of short stories, four collections of poetry, three plays and three essays. Stevenson died of a brain haemorrhage in 1894 aged 44 years, leaving five incomplete works.

A Summary of the Key Events in the Plot

Dr Jekyll and Mr Hyde is a novella (a short novel) concerned with the new scientific theories of the late Victorian age and the conflict of these with religion, plus the dual nature of mankind, or the capacity of human beings for good and evil.

Dr Henry Jekyll is a respectable, middle-class medical doctor. He also has an interest in new scientific discoveries and conducts experiments* which allow him to transform himself into his alter ego, the evil and violent Mr Edward Hyde, who refuses to accept responsibility for his actions and repent. Jekyll can control Hyde for a while, but as the novella progresses Hyde becomes more and more dominant and controlling of Jekyll. Hyde's violent dominance eventually leads to the death of Dr Jekyll and Mr Hyde.

The novella begins with two men, Mr Gabriel Utterson the lawyer and Jekyll's friend, and Mr Richard Enfield, Utterson's cousin, taking a walk together in London. They come to a strange, neglected building which is two storeys high but has no windows and a door with no bell or knocker. The building is attached to Jekyll's house. Enfield tells Utterson the tale of Mr Hyde trampling a young girl without showing any remorse for his actions. Utterson is intrigued, especially as he learns that Jekyll, his client, associates with Hyde so he decides to watch the door and try and speak to Hyde.

Finally, Utterson meets Hyde and is shocked and repulsed by him. He decides to visit Jekyll to warn him about Hyde. Jekyll is not at home, but his butler Poole advises Utterson that Hyde has a key to Jekyll's laboratory and Jekyll has ordered his servants to allow Hyde to come and go as he wishes.

Two weeks later, Utterson meets Jekyll at a dinner party and asks him about his involvement with Hyde. Jekyll laughs off Utterson's concern that Hyde is the benefactor of Jekyll's will and tells Utterson not to mention it again.

Nearly a year later, the elderly MP Sir Danvers Carew is brutally murdered by Hyde using Jekyll's walking cane. Utterson is determined Hyde should be brought to justice for his actions. Following the murder, Jekyll initially becomes withdrawn but reassures his friends that he is no longer in contact with Hyde. After time Jekyll returns to his old self and all is well. However, this is not to last as Jekyll eventually becomes depressed and refuses to see Utterson, who in turn visits Dr Hastie Lanyon, an old college friend of Jekyll's. A believer in traditional forms of medicine, Lanyon has no patience with Jekyll's scientific experiments* and has had limited contact with Jekyll for roughly ten years. After secretly witnessing Dr Jekyll transform into Mr Hyde at the former's request, Lanyon dies from shock and illness and hands Utterson a letter with the instruction that it is not to be opened until after Jekyll's death.

Poole then visits Utterson one evening asking for help as he can hear strange noises and an unfamiliar voice coming from Jekyll's laboratory. Utterson and Poole break down the door to find Hyde wearing Jekyll's clothes. He is writhing on the floor and near death as he has swallowed a phial of arsenic. Utterson and Poole also find Jekyll's will on a table with Hyde's name crossed out and Utterson's inserted in its place. There is also a confession, written by Jekyll. Utterson takes these documents home with him and reads them along with Lanyon's letter which describes him witnessing Jekyll turning into Hyde. He also reads Jekyll's confession which describes his experiments in detail and the gradual domination of Jekyll by Hyde which ultimately reveals the dual nature of man.

Form in *The Strange Case of Dr Jekyll and Mr Hyde*

Gothic Fiction and *The Strange Case of Dr Jekyll and Mr Hyde*

Jekyll and Hyde has its origins in Gothic literature, a genre which originated in the eighteenth century and which has a number of distinguishing features. Gothic novels are usually set in the past, with a sinister and creepy tone, and often set in castles, derelict buildings or faraway places. Stevenson's novella departs from the conventions of Gothic literature in several ways. Firstly, *Jekyll and Hyde* is set in an identifiable place, London, and in the present. This suggests that Stevenson proposes London to be a strange, frightening place in which there is untold secrecy, and nothing is as it seems.

Sensation Fiction

Sensation fiction of the 1860s was closely related to and derived from the Gothic. It was centred in everyday reality, but strange situations were created to provide a sense of the weird and sinister within the familiar. As such, sensation fiction was melodramatic and unsettling.

A structural feature of sensationalist narratives is that they make use of diaries, letters, individual commentaries and written confessions. Some of these appear in *Jekyll and Hyde*; for example, the sensationalist newspaper reporting of Carew's murder, Lanyon's letter, Jekyll's will and confession. These devices and Stevenson's use of the first person in each of the individual narratives gives pace and immediacy to the whole text. Personal narratives lend credibility and a sense of melodrama, whilst the title of each of the narratives draws attention to their personal nature.

Finally, the full title of Stevenson's novella, *The Strange Case of Dr Jekyll and Mr Hyde* suggests the narrative is informed by legal and medical knowledge. Stevenson, as we have seen, was a qualified lawyer and he also had a great interest in medical advances at the time, especially the development of psychoanalysis and theories about criminology. This knowledge is emphasised by the inclusion of characters from both professions in the novella – Mr Utterson the lawyer and Dr Jekyll and Dr Lanyon. The connotations of the word 'case' also indicate that *Jekyll and Hyde* can be considered a detective novel with a mystery to solve. Detective fiction was especially enjoyed during the Victorian era, most notably in the stories by Sir Arthur Conan Doyle and his famous detective, Sherlock Holmes.

Dr Jekyll and Mr Hyde

25 Key Quotations for GCSE

Quotation 1

Chapter 1: Story of the Door

"Mr Utterson the lawyer was a man of rugged countenance, that was never lighted by a smile; […] lean, long, dusty, dreary, and yet somehow lovable. He was austere with himself; […] and though he enjoyed the theatre, had not crossed the doors of one for twenty years. But he had an approved tolerance for others."

Analysis

Mr Gabriel Utterson is the main narrator in the novella. He is tall, thin, 'dusty and dreary' which indicates he is unimaginative and dull. However, as a middle-class lawyer and respectable member of Victorian society, Stevenson presents him as a reliable and trustworthy character who represents the model gentleman. As a serious and sombre character whose face was 'never lighted by a smile', Mr Utterson is also calm and unremarkable which allows the reader to focus on his narrative perspective, rather than his character.

Mr Utterson is also used to juxtapose Dr Henry Jekyll's refusal to follow society's rules as Jekyll gives into his desires, such as violence, through the creation of Mr Edward Hyde. Contrastingly, Mr Utterson places his reputation* and acting morally above anything else and ignoring activities he enjoys, such as going to the theatre. Mr Utterson is restrained and always acts as a gentleman was expected to behave. Underneath Mr Utterson's 'austere' exterior and manner, however, lies a man who is humane and tolerant of the mistakes of others and their misfortunes. It is this tolerance and concern which leads him to pursue a search for Mr Hyde as he is concerned that Jekyll is a victim of blackmail by Mr Hyde. In his pursuit of Mr Hyde, Mr Utterson is portrayed as curious, fair-minded, judicious and astute, demonstrating all the qualities of a good lawyer.

Key Characters
Mr Utterson

Key Themes
Reputation

Quotation 2

Chapter 1: Story of the Door

"The man trampled calmly over the child's body and left her screaming on the ground. It sounds nothing to hear, but it was hellish to see. It wasn't like a man; it was like some damned Juggernaut."

Analysis

This quotation occurs when Mr Enfield gives an account to Mr Utterson of when he witnessed Hyde deliberately trampling a young girl in the street. The most striking and disturbing aspects of Mr Enfield's account are the apparently deliberate assault of a small child by Hyde and the callous, calm manner with which he tramples her before continuing on his way. The use of semi-colons, commas and the list-like structure of this quotation give a sense of the suddenness and continuity of Mr Hyde's movements and the way in which he completely disregards the child. It is the reader's first experience of Mr Hyde's complete lack of morals.

Mr Enfield asserts that although it sounds 'nothing to hear' when he recalls the incident, it was 'hellish to see'. Mr Enfield's reference to Hell suggests Mr Hyde's actions are beyond the realms of civilised behaviour and are immoral, cruel and criminal. The simile 'like some damned Juggernaut' suggests Mr Hyde's behaviour is inhuman. 'Juggernaut' is usually used to describe a large, forceful object. Originally a Hindu god, worshippers of Juggernaut would display their devotion by throwing themselves in front of a vehicle carrying an image of the god in a procession. The simile has the effect of Mr Hyde's superhuman power and strength as he relentlessly ploughs over the girl with complete disregard for her welfare. The use of 'damned' could also suggest that Stevenson's text is written from the perspective that Christianity and western culture were seen to be superior to other religions and cultures. Whilst an unacceptable view today, the use of racially informed language was acceptable in the Victorian era, especially in relation to cultures and nations subjugated by British imperial rule.

Key Characters

Mr Edward Hyde
Mr Richard Enfield

Key Themes

Dual nature of man
Evolution

Quotation 3

Chapter 1: Story of the Door

"We told the man we could and would make such a scandal out of this, as should make his name stink from one end of London to the other […]

"'If you choose to make capital out of this accident,' said he, 'Name your figure.'"

Analysis

This quotation occurs in the aftermath of Mr Hyde's trampling down of the young girl and describes the reactions of the bystanders. The emphasis in this quotation is upon reputation and blackmail. Mr Enfield asserts they will create such a scandal out of the incident that Mr Hyde's name will be notorious across London and he will be socially and financially ruined. Mr Hyde responds by accusing the bystanders of making 'capital' or financial gain from the 'accident'. His use of the noun 'accident' indicates he refuses to accept responsibility for his actions and it is only to save his reputation that he agrees to pay compensation. The concern with maintaining one's reputation was clearly of paramount importance to middle-class Victorian men. Whilst Mr Hyde's social position is often unclear, as he later asserts, any gentleman 'wishes to avoid a scene'.

However, the means used to maintain respectability is a rather unscrupulous one – blackmail. A double standard is evident here as an illegal act is used to maintain reputation rather than through the legal and judicial system of the courts. The respectable veneer of Victorian society is exposed as corrupt. Mr Hyde agrees to pay £100 compensation to the girl's family, which was a large sum in the Victorian period. Mr Hyde goes to the back entrance of Dr Jekyll's house, enters, and then returns with a cheque signed by Dr Jekyll. In doing so, Dr Jekyll's name and his financial and professional reputation is embroiled in Mr Hyde's criminality. It is no coincidence that there is pun on 'Hyde'/'hide' and the desire for Dr Jekyll to keep his violent, subversive persona hidden from public view, as his entire personal and professional integrity hinges upon his reputation as an upright, respectable member of society.

Key Characters	Key Themes
Mr Edward Hyde	Reputation
Mr Richard Enfield	Secrecy

Quotation 4

Chapter 1: Story of the Door

"I never saw a circle of such hateful faces; and there was the man in the middle, with a kind of black, sneering coolness – frightened too, [...] but carrying it off, sir, really like Satan."

Analysis

This quotation follows Mr Hyde's trampling of the young girl and the reaction of bystanders to his actions. The 'hateful faces' at the beginning of the quotation refers to a group of women who have gathered in a circle around Mr Hyde and are immensely angry at what he has done. Despite being in the midst of these women, Mr Hyde appears to be cool and composed. The adjectives used to describe Mr Hyde – 'black, sneering coolness' – suggest an arrogance about his demeanour and his refusal to accept any responsibility for his actions. He may feel frightened amidst the women due to his small stature, but his 'coolness' indicates his complete disregard for the opinions of others. Mr Hyde seems untouchable here, as though he exists completely outside society and is alien to it. This is furthered by comparing Mr Hyde to 'Satan', another name for the devil, rendering Hyde the personification of evil.

Furthermore, Stevenson emphasises Mr Hyde's evil nature to the reader by introducing this title of being Satan-like before we are provided with his name. This dehumanises* Mr Hyde and focuses our attention on his animal-like behaviour, rather than on his personality or qualities as a human.

Key Characters
Mr Edward Hyde

Key Themes
Dual Nature of man

Quotation 5

Chapter 2: Search for Mr Hyde

"This was a hearty, healthy, dapper, red-faced gentleman, with a shock of hair prematurely white, and a boisterous and decided manner. At sight of Mr Utterson, he sprang up from his chair and welcomed him with both hands."

Analysis

This quotation describes Dr Hastie Lanyon, a childhood friend of Dr Jekyll and Mr Utterson. He is presented as a confident, talkative, friendly and larger than life character. Lanyon, however, holds very definite views, especially regarding new scientific advances. He disagrees with Dr Jekyll's type of experimentation and considers it to be unscientific and unethical, stating that it is 'unscientific balderdash' – meaning that it is nonsense. So much so, that he has broken his friendship with Dr Jekyll and has very little to do with him.

When Dr Lanyon witnesses Dr Jekyll's transformation into Mr Hyde it traumatises him so deeply that he does not recover, has a fit and dies.

Dr Lanyon represents the respectable doctor accepted in Victorian society. He respects tradition and follows the religious doctrine* of Christianity. He is used by Stevenson to highlight how different Jekyll's views are when compared with the stereotypical way that Dr Lanyon behaves.

Key Characters

Dr Hastie Lanyon

Key Themes

Dual nature of man
Evolution
Science

Quotation 6

Chapter 2: Search for Mr Hyde

"'But it is more than ten years since Henry Jekyll became too fanciful for me. He began to go wrong, wrong in mind; […] I have seen devilish little of the man. Such unscientific balderdash,' […] 'would have estranged Damon and Pythias.'"

Analysis

This quotation occurs early in the novella when Mr Utterson visits Dr Lanyon to ask him if he knows anything of Dr Jekyll's connection with Mr Hyde. Dr Lanyon reveals that although as an old friend he is concerned for Dr Jekyll's welfare, he has little time for Dr Jekyll's type of scientific experiments which he views as 'fanciful'. Dr Lanyon's choice of adjective indicates he considers Dr Jekyll to be dabbling in a dangerous, mystical form of science which could lead to disastrous results. Dr Lanyon also suggests there has been a change in Dr Jekyll's mental state: 'He began to go wrong, wrong in mind,' implying that Dr Jekyll must be insane to attempt such experiments. Dr Lanyon describes Jekyll's work as 'unscientific balderdash', or rubbish, as it does not accord with or follow the processes of mainstream science and as such is fundamentally flawed. The continued motif of evil also appears when Dr Lanyon uses the phrase 'devilish'. Whilst he means that it has been difficult to meet with his friend, Dr Lanyon is also unwittingly reinforcing the idea to the reader that Dr Jekyll is involved with evil deeds.

The reference to Damon and Pythias is a Greek legend in which two friends came to symbolise the willingness to sacrifice oneself for a friend. Whilst there are differing versions of the story, the best known are based on one of the two friends being condemned to death and he asks to be granted time to put his affairs in order. This request is refused until his friend offers to die in his place if he does not return. When the condemned man returns, his captor is moved by their friendship and so frees them both. In the context of Dr Lanyon's reference, he is implying that Dr Jekyll's experiments are so frightful and appalling that no friend would offer to sacrifice themselves for him but would leave him to suffer and continue alone.

Key Characters
Dr Hastie Lanyon

Key Themes
Science

Quotation 7

Chapter 2: Search for Mr Hyde

"Mr Hyde was pale and dwarfish, he gave an impression of deformity without any nameable malformation, he had a displeasing smile, [...] he spoke with a husky, whispering and somewhat broken voice; [...] but not all of these together could explain the hitherto unknown disgust, loathing, and fear with which Mr Utterson regarded him."

Analysis

This quotation follows Mr Utterson's first meeting with Mr Hyde and describes the effect Mr Hyde has upon him. Mr Hyde is described using negative and sinister language. He is 'pale and dwarfish', gives 'an impression of deformity' and has a 'displeasing smile', creating a character who is shifty and inhuman. Indeed, even his voice is 'husky', 'whispering' and 'broken', indicating an inability or unwillingness to speak clearly which suggests that he has a deeper, darker secret. Mr Hyde is deformed without any 'nameable malformation', indicating his deformities are unmentionable in civilised society. This reference is characteristic of Gothic literature and increases the sense of mystery and horror in the passage. Gothic literature usually includes a figure who is an outsider in society. Mr Enfield reacts to Mr Hyde in a negative manner, feeling only 'disgust' and 'loathing' for him. Mr Utterson struggles to put his thoughts into words and cannot define exactly why he finds Mr Hyde so unsettling.

Mr Hyde's lack of communication hints at his inexperience. He is regularly referred to as being 'young' and having recently been created, there is a sense that whilst he is evil, Mr Hyde simply does not have any experience dealing with other people. Although Dr Jekyll has, as he says, 'a great, a very great interest in that young man', he fails to educate his creation about the morality* of right and wrong. This is similar to the issues faced in Mary Shelley's Gothic novel *Frankenstein*, first published in 1818. It tells the tale of the talented scientist Victor Frankenstein who experiments with dead bodies and eventually creates a hideous monster that he goes on to reject. Initially having no education or understanding of the world, the monster educates himself and eventually takes revenge on those who rejected him, killing members of Frankenstein's family in the process. It is a cautionary tale about the dangers of experimenting with science and of trying to play God. Given that *Frankenstein* was published almost seventy years before *The Strange Case of Dr Jekyll and Mr Hyde*, Stevenson's very similar warning demonstrates the fear that many Victorians held about the rise of scientific discovery across the nineteenth century.

Key Characters
Mr Edward Hyde
Mr Richard Enfield

Key Themes
Dual nature of man
Evolution
Science

Quotation 8

Chapter 2: Search for Mr Hyde

"God bless me, the man seems hardly human!
Something troglodytic, shall we say?"

Analysis

This quotation occurs after Utterson has met Hyde for the first time and feels rather unsettled as he cannot define Hyde in human terms. Eventually he defines Hyde as 'something troglodytic' or with the characteristics of early man. Anthropoid apes such as gorillas and chimpanzees are also classified as troglodytes, indicating that Hyde, like many other primates, exhibits human characteristics whilst not being entirely human. The use of 'troglodytic' draws upon Victorian scientific advances. In 1859 the biologist and naturalist Charles Darwin published his work *The Origin of Species* in which he outlined his theory of evolution or survival of the fittest through natural selection. In 1871 Darwin refined his evolutionary theories further in *The Descent of Man* and caused further scandal when he proposed that humans are descended from apes, the concept of which offended many prudish Victorians. In a society where religion was entrenched in everyday life, the notion of natural selection and the thought that humans had descended from apes, rather than being created by God, was shocking. Indeed, Darwin did not publish *The Origin of Species* for twenty years as he knew his ideas would cause a huge uproar.

The growth of the British empire from the mid-sixteenth century onwards and the discovery of the 'New World', such as the Americas, led to an increased British awareness of other races and cultures and gave birth to anthropology*. Many anthropological works were published throughout the Victorian period which were essentially scientific observations of the culture of colonised people. In order to legitimise empire however, the superiority of white European races was established, with other races lower down the social and evolutionary scale. Anthropologists argued that there were three evolutionary stages in the formation of culture and that different races and classes of people were indicative of each stage. The three stages were: 1) **Savagery:** represented by Native American Indians, African races and tribes. 2) **Barbarism:** represented by peasants and other rustics, including the working class and criminals. 3) **Civilisation:** represented by the church and universities or educated Europeans. Such blatant racism and class subjugation is reiterated in Stevenson's presentation of Hyde as 'troglodytic'. Stevenson's imagery places Hyde lower down on the evolutionary scale. Hyde is presented as primitive*, deformed in some way and with a limited capacity for language as he can only whisper in a 'broken voice'. Although this presentation of Hyde reflects Victorian anthropology, what would have been more disturbing to the Victorian reader is that Hyde is present within Jekyll's psyche*. Stevenson's presentation of the Jekyll/Hyde dual personality proposes that primitivism is not as far removed from the educated, middle classes in Britain as members of that class would prefer to think and was much closer to 'civilised' society than had previously been acknowledged.

Key Characters	Key Themes
Mr Edward Hyde	Dual nature of man
Mr Utterson	Evolution

Quotation 9

Chapter 2: Search for Mr Hyde

"He was wild when he was young; a long while ago to be sure; […] Ay, it must be that; the ghost of some old sin, the cancer of some concealed disgrace: punishment coming, PEDE CLAUDO, years after memory has forgotten and self-love condoned the fault."

Analysis

This quotation, spoken by Mr Utterson, follows his meeting with Mr Hyde, during which Mr Utterson felt very threatened and unsettled at Mr Hyde's odd manner and peculiar, almost inhuman appearance. He decides to visit Dr Jekyll and warn him about his association with Mr Hyde, but when he does so, he finds that Dr Jekyll is not at home. Instead, Mr Utterson speaks to Dr Jekyll's butler, Poole, who advises him that Mr Hyde has a key to Dr Jekyll's laboratory and has been given permission by Dr Jekyll to come and go as he pleases. Mr Utterson considers Dr Jekyll's trust in Mr Hyde to be misplaced and wonders what kind of trouble he is in.

Mr Utterson's thoughts, spoken aloud in this quotation, suggest that Dr Jekyll was lively and rebellious when he was young compared to his present-day image of a respectable doctor. This is not especially unusual, but Mr Utterson continues by referencing religious laws and the sinful nature of humanity. In this Calvinist doctrine* humans are inherently evil unless they are able to repent sufficiently of their past sins and be saved by God. Otherwise, as this quotation suggests, justice will follow, even if it is at a much later date, and will arrive '*pede claudo*' (or limping behind). Mr Utterson's citation of this Calvinist doctrine raises the wider theme of the dual nature of man and mankind's capacity for good and evil, which is personified in the figures of Dr Jekyll and Mr Hyde.

The interest in the duality of human nature reflects the emerging Victorian sciences of psychiatry, criminology and sexology which developed into the psychiatric and psychological theories of today. As such, Stevenson's text can be viewed as experimental and indicative of the new scientific theories of the time.

Key Characters

Dr Henry Jekyll
Mr Utterson

Key Themes

Dual nature of man
Science versus religion

Quotation 10

Chapter 2: Search for Mr Hyde

"This Mister Hyde, if he were studied," thought he, "must have secrets of his own: black secrets compared to which poor Jekyll's worst would be like sunshine."

Analysis

This quotation occurs after Mr Utterson has met Mr Hyde by the back doorway to Dr Jekyll's home. Mr Utterson has felt very unsettled following his exchange with Mr Hyde and feels that Mr Hyde must have sinister secrets. These secrets are 'black' suggesting evil and criminality and can also be interpreted to have racial connotations. Dr Jekyll's worst secrets in comparison seem as bright as the sun. This imagery of light and dark highlights the polar opposites of the dual nature of man displayed in Dr Jekyll and Mr Hyde. There is much irony in this quotation as Dr Jekyll's secrets are Mr Hyde's and vice versa.

Key Characters
Dr Henry Jekyll
Mr Edward Hyde
Mr Utterson

Key Themes
Dual nature of man
Evolution

Quotation 11

Chapter 3:
Dr Jekyll was Quite at Ease

"He now sat on the opposite side of the fire—a large, well-made, smooth-faced man of fifty, with something of a slyish cast perhaps, but every mark of capacity and kindness—you could see by his looks that he cherished for Mr Utterson a sincere and warm affection."

Analysis

This description of Henry Jekyll in the narrative voice portrays him as a tall, fairly well-built middle-aged man, who is intelligent and approachable. He clearly values his friends and is genuine in his fondness for Mr Utterson.

Despite these characteristics, however, Dr Jekyll has 'something of a slyish cast about him' which casts doubt on his respectability, indicating that he has a darker side and foreshadows the dual nature of Dr Jekyll and Mr Hyde later in the novella. This duplicity of Dr Jekyll's nature is reiterated later in this section of the text when Mr Utterson challenges him over his wisdom in making Hyde the beneficiary of his will. Dr Jekyll reacts sharply to Mr Utterson's advice and his face grows 'pale to the very lips, and there came a blackness about his eyes'. These physical changes in Dr Jekyll's appearance suggest a darker side to Dr Jekyll which surfaces when he is stressed or under pressure, indicating that his respectable, friendly demeanour is a façade masking a darker, more hostile character underneath. It is also another example of the physical effect that Mr Hyde has when he is seen or mentioned by other characters in the novella.

Key Characters
Dr Henry Jekyll

Key Themes
Dual nature of man
Evolution

Quotation 12

Chapter 3:
Dr Jekyll was Quite at Ease

"I never saw a man so distressed as you were by my will; unless it were that hide-bound pedant, Lanyon, at what he called my scientific heresies. [...] I was never more disappointed in any man than Lanyon.'"

Analysis

This quotation, spoken by Dr Jekyll, is in reply to Mr Utterson's concern about Dr Jekyll's relationship with Mr Hyde and his bequeathing of his wealth to Mr Hyde in his will. Dr Jekyll brushes Mr Utterson's concerns aside 'gaily' and the tone of his subsequent dialogue indicates that he rebuffs Mr Utterson with a self-assured, almost arrogant manner. This is confirmed as he calls Dr Lanyon 'a hide-bound pedant' which confirms the deep rift between both doctors. 'Hide-bound' is an old term derived from animal hide or leather, to mean someone who is inflexible and set in their opinions. It also puns on 'Hyde', who is literally bound to Dr Jekyll like his second skin. A 'pedant' is someone who enjoys displaying their knowledge and is very particular about factual accuracy.

Dr Jekyll recalls Dr Lanyon's reaction to his experiments as 'scientific heresies', using religious language to express scepticism regarding a branch of science. 'Heresy', especially in Christianity, is a belief or opinion that does not agree with religious doctrine. Dr Lanyon uses the language of conventional religious belief to question Dr Jekyll's unorthodox science and to propose that his science contradicts all current scientific ideas and practices. The language used also unites the themes of religious belief and science as Dr Jekyll's interest in evolution is contrary to the belief that God created the universe and everything in it, including mankind. Furthermore, Dr Jekyll's statement that he 'was never more disappointed in any man than Lanyon' suggests Dr Jekyll's science is not common and that he is disappointed by the traditional, unambitious views of science that men like Dr Lanyon held.

Key Characters
Dr Hastie Lanyon
Dr Henry Jekyll

Key Themes
Dual nature of man
Evolution
Science versus religion

Quotation 13

Chapter 4:
The Carew Murder Case

"Mr Hyde broke out of all bounds and clubbed him to the earth. And next moment, with ape-like fury, he was trampling his victim under foot and hailing down a storm of blows, under which the bones were audibly shattered and the body jumped upon the roadway."

Analysis

This quotation, in the narrative voice, vividly describes the murder of the elderly Sir Danvers Carew by Mr Hyde. The violent assault upon a weaker man is described using graphic language and a list structure to indicate the sustained attack on Sir Carew. Mr Hyde 'clubbed' Sir Carew to the ground before 'trampling' on him and subjecting him to a 'storm of blows' which are so excessive that the cracking of Sir Carew's bones can be heard, and his body jumps as Mr Hyde strikes each blow. The violence of the language suggests Mr Hyde's irrational ferocity, and indicates Sir Carew suffers a sustained attack. Mr Hyde 'breaks out of all bounds' of rational and civilised behaviour and assumes an 'ape-like fury' during the attack. The reference to apes dehumanises Mr Hyde and suggests that he is lower down the evolutionary scale, according to Victorian evolutionary and anthropological theory, and is the primitive version of his alter ego, Dr Jekyll. The criminality of Mr Hyde's actions is emphasised as he 'breaks all bounds' of civilised behaviour, indicating his blatant disregard for the law and preservation of human life. Therefore, Mr Hyde is presented as Dr Jekyll's racial and primitive other and is as far removed as anyone could be from the professional, middle-aged doctor who is concerned with preserving life, not taking it.

Key Characters
Mr Edward Hyde

Key Themes
Dual nature of man
Evolution

Quotation 14

Chapter 5:
Incident of the Letter

"If it came to a trial, your name might appear."

"I cannot say that I care what becomes of Hyde; I am quite done with him. I was thinking of my own character, which this hateful business has rather exposed."

Analysis

This quotation follows the murder of Sir Carew when Mr Utterson visits Dr Jekyll to ask him if he is hiding Mr Hyde. When Dr Jekyll denies he is doing so, Mr Utterson warns him that he would not want his name to appear in any prospective criminal trial, with the implication that his reputation as a middle-class professional will be ruined if he is publicly seen to associate with Mr Hyde the murderer.

Dr Jekyll's response is rather self-centred. He claims he 'doesn't care' what happens to Mr Hyde and admits he is more concerned about his own reputation since if this is damaged, he will be unable to continue practicing as a doctor and his wealth and social standing will be lost. Dr Jekyll's denial of Mr Hyde also suggests that he is horrified by his murderous actions as Mr Hyde. His assertion that he does not care what becomes of Mr Hyde is an attempt to repress his primitive self in favour of his evolved, civilised self.

Key Characters	Key Themes
Dr Henry Jekyll	Dual nature of man
Mr Utterson	Evolution
	Reputation
	Secrecy

Quotation 15

Chapter 6:
Remarkable Incident of Dr Lanyon

"PRIVATE: for the hands of G. J. Utterson ALONE and in case of his predecease *to be destroyed unread*"

Analysis

This note is written on the envelope of a letter written by Dr Lanyon before his death with the instruction that it is to be opened only by Mr Utterson. Within the envelope is another enclosure with the instruction 'not to be opened until after the death or disappearance of Dr Henry Jekyll'. The use of the word 'PRIVATE' written in capital letters highlights the theme of secrecy in the novel and suggests that some facts are only accessible to certain people, in this case, Mr Utterson. The fact it is Mr Utterson 'ALONE' (again in capitals) indicates he is the only person entrusted with the truth of Dr Jekyll's case and if he predeceases Dr Jekyll then the truth of the affair will always remain secret. The use of italics in the quotation emphasises the secrecy surrounding the affair.

Key Characters
Dr Hastie Lanyon
Mr Utterson

Key Themes
Reputation
Secrecy

Quotation 16

Chapter 8: The Last Night

"Utterson was amazed to find [...] a copy of a pious work, for which Jekyll had several times expressed a great esteem, annotated, in his own hand, with startling blasphemies."

Analysis

This quotation, in the narrative voice, occurs in the novella when Poole, Dr Jekyll's butler, visits Mr Utterson one evening as he is concerned for Dr Jekyll's welfare. Dr Jekyll has been shut up in his laboratory for days and Poole has heard strange noises coming from the room. Mr Utterson goes with Poole to Dr Jekyll's house and they force the door of the laboratory open. Inside they find Mr Hyde dressed in Dr Jekyll's clothes and writhing on the floor close to death. He has evidently swallowed a phial of arsenic.

They cannot find Dr Jekyll and proceed to go through his belongings for clues. Mr Utterson notices a copy of a 'pious work', indicating a religious-themed book which Dr Jekyll had formerly admired. Now, however, the book has been annotated with 'startling blasphemies'. To be blasphemous one shows disrespect to a god or religion either by words or actions. In annotating the pious work with blasphemous phrases, Dr Jekyll rejects Christianity and its doctrines, exacerbating his isolation from conventional society as Mr Hyde takes over. The blasphemy is written in Dr Jekyll's hand rather than Mr Hyde's and confirms not just their dual nature but also the extent to which Mr Hyde has supremacy over the 'civilised' Dr Jekyll.

Key Characters	Key Themes
Dr Henry Jekyll	Dual nature of man
Mr Edward Hyde	Evolution
Mr Utterson	Science versus religion

Quotation 17

Chapter 9:
Dr Lanyon's Narrative

"Lanyon, you remember your vows […] And now, you who have so long been bound to the most narrow and material views, you who have denied the virtue of transcendental medicine, you who have derided your superiors—behold!"

Analysis

This quotation forms part of Dr Lanyon's narrative and occurs when Mr Hyde visits Dr Lanyon and transforms himself back into Dr Jekyll before Dr Lanyon's eyes to prove his experiments to the sceptical Dr Lanyon. The quotation refers to the 'vows' taken by both of them, meaning the oath that doctors took upon graduating in medicine. Mr Hyde seemingly makes a mistake here and speaks as Dr Jekyll, although his slip could also indicate the merging of both their egos. Mr Hyde asserts that Dr Lanyon has been 'bound' to the 'narrow and material views' of medicine and has refused to accept new branches of medicine such as 'transcendental medicine' with its roots in evolutionary theory. The adjective 'transcendental' implies a mystical form of medicine unrooted in fact. Dr Jekyll's experiment has certainly produced the mystical figure of Mr Hyde as he cannot be described or understood using familiar every day or scientific contexts. Mr Hyde defies description. This implies that Dr Jekyll's science transcends all previous scientific theory. He considers the practitioners of contemporary science to be ordinary and mundane. In contrast the new 'superior' scientists like himself have opened up new frontiers and explorations of the origins of humankind and what it actually means to be human. Mr Hyde plays the part of the mystic too by using the dramatic and imperative "behold!", as though he is a magician performing a logic-defying trick.

Key Characters

Dr Hastie Lanyon

Mr Edward Hyde

Key Themes

Dual nature of man

Evolution

Science versus religion

Quotation 18

Chapter 10: Henry Jekyll's Full Statement of the Case

"And indeed the worst of my faults was a certain impatient gaiety of disposition, […] but such as I found it hard to reconcile with my imperious desire to carry my head high, and wear a more than commonly grave countenance before the public. […] I concealed my pleasures; […] I thus drew steadily nearer to that truth, by whose partial discovery I have been doomed to such a dreadful shipwreck: that man is not truly one, but truly two."

Analysis

This quotation occurs at the beginning of 'Henry Jekyll's Full Statement of the Case' which forms the final chapter of the novella. Jekyll begins his narrative by asserting that he has always been aware that he has two definite but conflicting strands to his character. The first is described as an 'impatient gaiety of disposition' and indicates a private desire for pleasures (possibly sexual) which are frowned upon by respectable Victorian society, plus a tendency to live in the moment and act impulsively. The second aspect of his character is 'a more than commonly grave countenance' which suggests a dignified, rigid adherence to the strict moral codes of middle-class Victorian society and is perceived by Jekyll as fitting for the public face of a professional person. The fact that Jekyll adopts this countenance in public reflects his intense struggle to control his livelier and impulsive self. Jekyll feels ashamed about enjoying his natural impulses and frustrated at having to subdue them in favour of an artificial veneer to enable him to progress financially and socially. The more he observes his own dual nature from a scientific perspective, the more Jekyll starts to believe that all human beings have a dual nature – an impulsive natural being fighting against an identity formulated by the rigid demands of society. Jekyll concludes that 'man is not truly one but two'. The private and public personas Jekyll identifies are frequently in conflict with each other, indicating a divided self.

The theme of a dual personality in *Jekyll and Hyde* reflects the growth of psychology and psychiatry during the Victorian period, with its parallels to Sigmund Freud, who initially argued that our minds are made up of three elements; the conscious (events we are aware of), the preconscious (thoughts that are beginning to become conscious), and the unconscious (thoughts that we are not aware of). This theory would eventually become the concept of the id (our instinctual desires – the mode Hyde mostly operates in), the ego (the balance between the id and the super-ego – why Jekyll creates Hyde), and the super-ego (our morals – what frustrates Jekyll). Whilst this theory came after the publication of *Jekyll and Hyde,* it provides an insight into psychological thinking and development during the latter Victorian era.

Key Characters
Dr Henry Jekyll

Key Themes
Dual nature of man
Evolution

Quotation 19

Chapter 10: Henry Jekyll's Full Statement of the Case

"I was driven to reflect deeply and inveterately on that hard law of life, which lies at the root of religion and is one of the most plentiful springs of distress. [...] And it chanced that the direction of my scientific studies, which led wholly toward the mystic and the transcendental, re-acted and shed a strong light on this consciousness of the perennial war among my members."

Analysis

Dr Jekyll describes the conflict he feels within himself in this quotation and the burden of guilt and mental distress that religion and society places on him.

Through his unorthodox scientific experiments, Dr Jekyll discovers that the burden of guilt conflicts with mankind's natural, primitive instinct. This conflict causes continuous war and anguish within Dr Jekyll's mind as his developed, civilised self, represented by Christianity, and his natural, primitive instinct represented by his desires, fight for control of each other.

This conflict is fully manifested in the deaths of both Dr Jekyll and Mr Hyde, as the constraints of a rigid society ultimately override and reject unconventional and innovative ideas of identity and self.

Key Characters	Key Themes
Dr Henry Jekyll	Dual nature of man
	Evolution
	Science versus religion

Quotation 20

Chapter 10: Henry Jekyll's Full Statement of the Case

"It was on the moral side, and in my own person, that I learned to recognise the thorough and primitive duality of man; I saw that, of the two natures that contended in the field of my consciousness, even if I could rightly be said to be either, it was only because I was radically both"

Analysis

In this quotation Dr Jekyll explains that it was when his 'moral side' was prevalent that he reasoned that there are two aspects to the character of mankind within his and every human being's consciousness. Dr Jekyll acknowledges that both aspects of the dual personality are equal parts of the mind.

It is notable that it is when his 'moral' side is prevalent that Dr Jekyll is able to make his scientific observations, indicating rational thought. This suggests his alter ego, Mr Hyde, constitutes the irrational, spontaneous aspect of his psyche. This irrationality is associated with the instinctive, impulsive and uncontrollable, primitive behaviour, such as Mr Hyde's trampling of the young girl and his 'ape-like fury' when he murders Sir Carew.

Once Dr Jekyll has identified the dual nature of man, he fantasises about separating the two aspects of his mind and begins his scientific experimentation with disastrous results.

Key Characters	Key Themes
Dr Henry Jekyll	Dual nature of man Evolution

Quotation 21

Chapter 10: Henry Jekyll's Full Statement of the Case

"Edward Hyde was so much smaller, slighter, and younger than Henry Jekyll. Even as good shone upon the countenance of the one, evil was written broadly and plainly on the face of the other. Evil [...] had left on that body an imprint of deformity and decay. And yet when I looked upon that I was conscious of no repugnance, rather of a leap of welcome. This, too, was myself. It seemed natural and human."

Analysis

In this quotation Jekyll outlines how he feels about his dual personality. He describes Hyde to be much smaller and younger than himself suggesting he considers Hyde to be an earlier, less developed and evolved version of himself as a middle-aged man. He contrasts the appearances of his two selves: good shines upon Jekyll's face, whereas evil darkens Hyde's features. Jekyll confirms this as he says 'evil' had left 'deformity and decay' on Hyde, using the language of Victorian anthropologists to imply that his irrational, impulsive self is a product of the primitive origins of mankind and offends the sensibilities of modern, civilised society. Interestingly, Jekyll is not horrified by his evil persona. He proclaims that when he sees his reflection as Hyde in the mirror, he is not repulsed by what he sees, instead he welcomes it as it seems 'natural and human'. Jekyll's reaction to Hyde contrasts sharply to that of the characters who feel a sense of unease, disgust and fear when confronted by Hyde and recoil from him. It can be argued that Jekyll has a Darwinian understanding of evolution and rather than being repulsed by his primitive, animalistic self is fascinated by it. Jekyll welcomes Hyde as a much-needed relief and release from the rigid strictures of modern society which can only mould and repress individuals according to indicators of success such as wealth and social standing. Jekyll indicates that Hyde represents the essence of humanity as it is a 'livlier image of the spirit', paring back human nature to its earliest forms. In the context of a society with such rigid religious and moral codes, Jekyll's discovery is immensely liberating.

Key Characters
Dr Henry Jekyll
Mr Edward Hyde

Key Themes
Dual nature of man
Evolution

Quotation 22

Chapter 10: Henry Jekyll's Full Statement of the Case

"Now the hand of Henry Jekyll [...] was professional in shape and size: it was large, firm, white and comely. But the hand which I now saw [...] was lean, corded, knuckly, of a dusky pallor and thickly shaded with a smart growth of hair. It was the hand of Edward Hyde."

Analysis

This quotation describes the time when Jekyll went to bed as himself but wakes as Hyde. It is a pivotal point in Jekyll's narrative as it signifies the moment when Jekyll starts to lose control of his primitive self (Hyde) and Hyde takes over the civilised, evolved Jekyll. As Jekyll wakes, he notices his hand in the early morning light. He observes that his hands are usually 'professional in shape and size' and 'large, white and comely'. The adjectives used to describe Jekyll's hands suggest they are firm and confident in their grip, and large, dexterous and capable. Furthermore, his hands are 'white and comely', drawing attention to the colour of his skin and the overall attractiveness of his hands.

This particular morning, however, Jekyll notices that his hands have undergone a transformation. They are now 'lean, corded, knuckly'. The rule of three emphasises the contrast between the previous description of Jekyll's hands, indicating roughness and deformity. Most strikingly is the difference in their colour – Jekyll's are 'white and comely' whilst Hyde's have a 'dusky pallor' and a 'smart growth of hair'. The imagery used to describe the colour and texture of Hyde's hands could easily be used to describe the hand of an ape. This ape-like imagery has racial connotations and indicates that Hyde is being presented as an earlier, less evolved species of modern man or as an ape. Bearing in mind the evolutionary and anthropological theories of the time, the contrasting imagery of Jekyll and Hyde's hands present Hyde as lower down the evolutionary scale than Jekyll and suggest Hyde either represents an ape or one of the 'lower' races of man, such as African tribespeople. To the modern reader this is extremely racist and offensive, and rightly so, but Victorian anthropology positioned white European males at the top of civilisation with white women, children and criminals following behind. Lagging behind this second group were other supposedly inferior or less developed races. It is interesting, however, that in a text underpinned by the racial inequality prevalent in much of the scientific theory of the time, that Jekyll's racial or primitive 'other' Hyde, gradually takes control of Jekyll. Could Stevenson be implying that such stereotypical and prejudicial connotations of race may one day topple the white European male from his lofty position at the top of civilisation?

Key Characters
Dr Henry Jekyll
Mr Edward Hyde

Key Themes
Dual nature of man
Evolution

Quotation 23

Chapter 10: Henry Jekyll's Full Statement of the Case

"My devil had been long caged, he came out roaring."

Analysis

This quotation occurs in Dr Jekyll's account of events when he realises that Mr Hyde could easily become uncontrollable and seeks to repress Mr Hyde through a simple lifestyle with regular habits, surrounded by his old friends. Despite this, Dr Jekyll does not discard Mr Hyde's old clothes, nor does he give up Mr Hyde's house in Soho, London, an area notoriously associated with brothels and prostitution in the Victorian era. Dr Jekyll's refusal to disregard the trappings associated with Mr Hyde indicates that he remains an intrinsic part of Dr Jekyll's persona which he cannot ignore.

Additionally, 'My devil had long been caged' is a metaphor that suggests Mr Hyde is like a zoo or circus animal such as a lion, imprisoned in a small, repressive cage and when he is released gives full vent to his wild, animalistic frustrations when he comes out 'roaring'. The metaphor of the cage also indicates sexual repression enforced by respectable Victorian society, but also raises a double standard as many 'respectable' middle-class men at the time frequented brothels. Earlier in his account Dr Jekyll admits that he enjoyed certain pleasures with 'almost a morbid sense of shame'. It is notable that the nature of these pleasures remain unnamed, but Victorian prudery and censorship of literary texts would have prevented any overt reference to sexual matters.

The use of the noun 'devil' also has religious connotations as the devil is the antithesis of the Holy Spirit in Christianity. This implies that sexuality is deemed to be sinful and was repressed whilst the outward appearance of a chaste, virtuous life was considered to be respectable, even if it was the rather hypocritical veneer on a secretive life.

Key Characters
Dr Henry Jekyll
Mr Edward Hyde

Key Themes
Dual nature of man
Evolution

Quotation 24

Chapter 10: Henry Jekyll's Full Statement of the Case

"Henry Jekyll, with streaming tears of gratitude and remorse, had fallen upon his knees and lifted his clasped hands to God. The veil of self-indulgence was rent from head to foot, I saw my life as a whole: [...] from the days of childhood, when I had walked with my father's hand, and through the self-denying toils of my professional life, to arrive again and again, with the same sense of unreality, at the damned horrors of the evening."

Analysis

This quotation occurs during Jekyll's account of events and demonstrates the immense difficulty he has in controlling Hyde. It also raises the conflict between science and religion in the novella and is informed by Biblical references and Christian modes of behaviour. The transformation of Jekyll into Hyde is described using violent language such as 'tearing' and implies the physical and emotional trauma Jekyll feels when becoming Hyde. This violence is undercut by the metaphor 'the veil of self-indulgence'. This image suggests that Jekyll initially considers the animalistic and violent instincts displayed by Hyde to be a 'veil' or a light translucent covering over the deeper reality of human existence which is explained, understood and underpinned by religious belief. This indicates Jekyll attempts to control and restrain his natural instincts through religious belief and prays to God for redemption. As Jekyll prays, 'the veil of self-indulgence was rent from head to foot'. The use of 'rent', meaning to tear, recalls Hyde's baser instincts 'tearing' at Jekyll and suggests that religion, in this case Christianity, forces people to behave more appropriately. This is supported by the image of the tearing of the temple veil in the New Testament account of Jesus' crucifixion, which is believed by Christians to represent the removal of the barrier between God and man. Following the metaphoric tearing of the veil in this quotation, Jekyll has a vision of his two lives. The first is of his respectable upbringing led by the hand of his father (which could also imply the hand of God as a father) and his adult life bearing the 'self-denying toils' of his profession which demand dedication to his patients. The second, which he cannot escape, are the 'horrors' of the evening. Although Jekyll attempts to override these 'horrors' through prayer the images of his primitive instincts continue to torture him and suggest that Jekyll cannot face what he and Hyde have done. Jekyll cannot escape his natural instincts regardless of the social norms which are underpinned by religious doctrine. The combination of violent adjectives and religious language in this quotation articulate the intense pressure Jekyll is under and the depth, complexity and seriousness of his physical and psychological suffering.

Key Characters

Dr Henry Jekyll

Mr Edward Hyde

Key Themes

Dual nature of man

Evolution

Science versus religion

Quotation 25

Chapter 10: Henry Jekyll's Full Statement of the Case

"I began to be aware of a change in the temper of my thoughts, a greater boldness, a contempt of danger, a solution of the bonds of obligation. [...] my clothes hung formlessly on my shrunken limbs; the hand that lay on my knee was corded and hairy. I was once more Edward Hyde. A moment before I had been safe of all men's respect, wealthy, beloved —the cloth laying for me in the dining-room at home; and now I was the common quarry of mankind, hunted, houseless, a known murderer, thrall to the gallows."

Analysis

This quotation occurs after the murder of Carew in Jekyll's account. Jekyll explains how his transformation into Hyde begins with a change in his mental state causing him to act more recklessly and disregard danger. Jekyll asserts that this recklessness is a 'solution to the bonds of obligation', suggesting that his alter ego provides a route to freedom from the oppressive bonds of civilised behaviour. Jekyll's mental change materialises in alterations to his physical appearance. He becomes smaller in stature, with 'shrunken limbs', and Jekyll's clothes are too big for him, hanging on him like a scarecrow. Once again, his hands assume an ape-like appearance and are 'corded and hairy'. This description is perhaps a warning from Stevenson about the challenges and dangers of experimental science, and of trying to – as Victorian society would have seen it – destroy and tamper with God's creation. This kind of science is generally used with the intention of progressing humanity, yet Jekyll's experiment – the creation of the 'ape-like' Hyde – degenerates* humanity, removing both any physical progression or moral sense of right and wrong.

Jekyll's physical and mental transformation has wider implications too. As Jekyll, he is the pillar of Victorian society. He is respected as a doctor and has the wealth associated with a middle-class professional. As such, he is 'beloved' by all around him and society at large. Jekyll upholds civilised values in its supposedly superior form – the white European middle-class male. The image of his dining table at home, complete with tablecloth, symbolises his status and respectability. In contrast to Jekyll's home comforts is Hyde's alienation from society. He is homeless so has no access to the symbols of wealth and respectability. Hyde has a well-known reputation as the worst type of criminal – he is a murderer. He is 'quarry' or prey of all mankind, destined to be pursued and hunted down. As such, he is 'thrall to the gallows' and the fear of discovery and execution is the only threat that has the power to control Hyde's actions.

Key Characters	Key Themes
Dr Henry Jekyll	Dual nature of man
Mr Edward Hyde	Evolution

Glossary of Key Terms

Anthropology: the study of human societies and their cultures and their development.

Degenerate: to become worse or weaker.

Dehumanise: to treat someone as if they are not human.

Calvinist doctrine: a set of Christian beliefs that is based on the teachings of John Calvin who believed in God's power and the moral weakness of human beings.

Morality: the belief about what is right and wrong.

Novella: a short novel.

Primitive: coming from an ancient time.

Psyche: the mind, personality and soul.

Religious doctrine: a set of religious ideas and beliefs to be taught and followed.

Repentance: to be sorry for something wrong that you have done and want to act in the right way in the future.

Reputation: the common view that is held about a person by others.

Scientific experiment: a procedure carried out to support, disprove, or verify a hypothesis (an unproven theory or idea).

Our fabulous new revision guides are out now!

25 Key Quotations for GCSE

- Romeo and Juliet
- A Christmas Carol
- Macbeth
- Dr Jekyll and Mr Hyde
- An Inspector Calls

GCSE Revision Guides

- An Inspector Calls
- A Christmas Carol
- Macbeth
- English Language

But that's not all! We've also got a host of annotation-friendly editions, containing oodles of space for you to fill with those all-important notes:

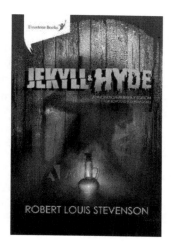

Annotation-Friendly Editions

- Dr Jekyll and Mr Hyde
- A Christmas Carol
- Romeo and Juliet
- Macbeth

... and lots more!

Available through Amazon, Waterstones, and all good bookshops!

About the author of this guide

Heather Hawkins is an English tutor and examiner for Cambridge, tutoring GCSE and A Level syllabi. She is also a director of The Thomas Hardy Association, based at the University of St Andrews. Heather has an ongoing research interest in Victorian Literature, specialising in Thomas Hardy, and researched dialect in Thomas Hardy's poetry for her doctoral thesis. During this research Heather recognised the necessity for students to adopt a socio-historical approach to their reading of literary texts to enable greater understanding and enjoyment of Literature. This concern supports the key quotations included in this guide to fully prepare students for the demands of the English Literature GCSE.

About the editor of this guide

Hannah Rabey is Head of English at a school in Oxfordshire. Hannah studied Literature and History at the University of East Anglia before studying for her PGCE at the University of Oxford. Hannah is a GCSE examiner and is experienced with teaching all of the texts in the 25 Key Quotations revision guide series.

Printed in Great Britain
by Amazon